BORDERS.
BOOKS MUSIC MOVIES CAFE

The NEW SAT:
Your Personalized Study Plan

A Borders Exclusive

By the Staff of Kaplan Test Prep and Admissions

Simon & Schuster

NEW YORK · LONDON · SYDNEY · TORONTO

Kaplan Publishing
Published by Simon & Schuster
1230 Avenue of the Americas
New York, NY 10020

Contributing Editors: Jon Zeitlin and Seppy Basili
Executive Editor: Jennifer Farthing
Project Editor: Sandy Gade
Production Manager: Michael Shevlin

September 2004
10 9 8 7 6 5 4 3 2 1

Manufactured in the United States of America
Published simultaneously in Canada

ISBN 0-7432-6984-5

For bulk sales, contact your local Borders store and ask to speak to the Corporate Sales Representative.

Table of Contents

HOW TO USE THIS GUIDE

This guide contains must-have information for learning about the new SAT and for getting the highest score possible. Each of the seven chapters will help you maximize your performance on the SAT, so consider each one an integral part of your SAT preparation.

Chapter One

Chapter one tells you about what to expect on the new SAT. It covers the changes from the old test to the new SAT, and gives you information about how the test is structured, when the test is given, and how the test is scored.

Chapter Two

This chapter is your true insider's guide to the new SAT. You will learn about which scores colleges are accepting, as well as the answers to the most important questions you may have about the new SAT.

Chapter Three

The new SAT has an essay writing section, and this chapter covers what you need to know about the essay. Learn about scoring and essay topics, and get practice writing your own SAT essay.

Chapter Four

The new SAT also has multiple-choice questions on the Writing section. Learn what types of question are found in this section. Practice with sample SAT questions and review your skills with detailed answer explanations.

Chapter Five

Want to learn about what is covered on the new SAT Critical Reading section? This chapter has important information about the passage types and the question types you will encounter. Get practice with sample questions, and review the answer explanations for more information.

Chapter Six

Chapter six covers the information you need to know about the new SAT Math section. You will learn about the math topics that are tested, as well as the two different question types: Grid-ins and multiple-choice questions. A set of practice questions complete with answer explanations will help you prepare.

Chapter Seven

Learn why a study group can be more effective than studying alone, who should join your group, what you should do to organize it, where you should meet, when to gather your group, and how to make your SAT study group a success.

Good luck!

Chapter One: **What to Expect on the New SAT**

CHANGES ON THE NEW SAT

To better reflect the kinds of skills required of college-bound students, the College Board—creator of the SAT I—has decided to change the SAT starting in March 2005. The new SAT will look very different from the current SAT, which has only two sections, Verbal and Math, and only multiple-choice and Grid-in questions. In contrast, the new test will have three sections: Critical Reading, Math, and Writing; it will include an essay; and it will be longer: 3 hours 45 minutes. To learn about the specific changes, let's take a look at the new SAT section by section.

Critical Reading

The Verbal section is now called Critical Reading. The College Board has dropped the analogy questions (no more *bird is to fly as fish is to…*) and they've added additional reading comprehension passages and questions. These new passages will be shorter than passages found on the current SAT. There will be 100-word paragraphs in addition to short, paired passages about related material in which questions will refer to one or both passages. Sentence Completion questions are still on the test.

Writing

The biggest change to the new SAT is the addition of a new section, Writing. This section is comprised of an essay and multiple-choice questions on grammar and usage. The new essay is the section that has been attracting the most attention and poses a big challenge. With 25-minutes to write an essay, you are not being tested on your ability to write a well-thought out multi-draft composition, you're being tested on how to write a first draft of an essay under extreme time pressure.

The College Board graders will be looking for a clearly constructed and well-organized essay without much care for creativity or the fine details of punctuation. You will be able to use some of the writing skills you've been developing at school over many years, but in addition, you are going to need to develop a new set of skills that will enable you stay calm and construct an essay that will get a high score.

You are probably aware that there is going to be an essay on the new SAT, but you may not realize that there will be a grammar section as well. Grammar will be worth nearly two-thirds of the overall 200–800 Writing score; this is equivalent to almost 20% of the overall SAT score.

Math

With the addition of algebra II on the new SAT, you will need methods and strategies to succeed on the math portion more than ever before. While the types of math questions will be more advanced, the reasoning and calculation methods won't change. The new SAT Math section will still include regular multiple-choice and Grid-in questions.

To see how each of the SAT sections is set up, including the time allotted, the types of questions, and the content tested, see the table on the following page.

The SAT sections are broken down like this:

Section	Length	Content	Type
Critical Reading	25 minutes	Sentence Completion and Reading Comprehension	Multiple-choice questions
Critical Reading	25 minutes	Sentence Completion and Reading Comprehension	Multiple-choice questions
Critical Reading	20 minutes	Sentence Completion and Reading Comprehension	Multiple-choice questions
Math	25 minutes	High school geometry and algebra, numbers and operations, statistics, probability, and data analysis	Multiple-choice questions and student-produced responses
Math	25 minutes	High school geometry and algebra, numbers and operations, statistics, probability, and data analysis	Multiple-choice questions and student-produced responses
Math	20 minutes	High school geometry and algebra, numbers and operations, statistics, probability, and data analysis	Multiple-choice questions and student-produced responses
Writing	25 minutes	Student-written essay	Long-form essay
Writing	35 minutes	Usage, Sentence Corrections, and Paragraph Corrections	Multiple-choice questions
Experimental (see note)	25 minutes	Math, Writing, or Critical Reading	Expect anything except an essay

Note: Every SAT has an experimental section. The experimental section is used by the test developers to try out new questions before including them in upcoming SATs. The experimental section DOES NOT COUNT in your score. It can show up anywhere on the exam and will look just like a normal section. You shouldn't try to figure out which SAT section is experimental. You will fail to do so. Treat all the sections as if they count toward your score.

Scoring the New Test

The new Writing section is scored on a scale of 200–800, as are the Math and Critical Reading sections. So, the composite (total) scores on the new SAT are 600–2400, instead of the 400–1600 on the old SAT. That means 1600 is no longer a perfect score—2400 is.

SAT TEST DATES

Because of all these changes, more students are taking the SAT earlier. There are two reasons for this:

- More students are applying to early decision programs.
- More students are taking the SAT more than once.

As a general rule, it's important to get SAT scores under your belt by the end of your junior year. That way, you know where you stand as you plan your college choices. Plus, it's likely that you'll improve your score by taking the exam a second time, since it will be familiar to you. The SAT is administered on select Saturdays during the school year. Sunday testing is available for students who cannot take the Saturday test because of religious observance. Here are the upcoming dates for the new SAT in 2005:

Test Date	Registration Deadlines U.S. and International	U.S. Late Registration
March 12, 2005	February 7, 2005	February 16, 2005
May 7, 2005	March 25, 2005	April 6, 2005
June 4, 2005	April 29, 2005	May 11, 2005

SAT FORMAT

The SAT is 3 hours and 45 minutes long, and there are two or three 10-minute breaks. The exam is mostly multiple-choice, and it's divided into three Math, three Critical Reading, and two Writing sections. These sections can appear in *any order* on test day; for example, you may get a test that starts with Critical Reading, then Writing, Math, Critical Reading, and so on. Or, your test could start with Math. The order is random and will be different from the order of the person sitting next to you.

HOW THE NEW SAT IS SCORED

You gain one point for each correct answer on the SAT and lose a fraction of a point (1/4 point, to be exact) for each wrong answer (except with Grid-ins, where you lose *nothing* for a wrong answer). You do not lose any points for questions you leave blank.

This is important, so we'll repeat it: **You do not lose *any* points for questions you leave blank.** The totals for the Critical Reading, Writing, and Math questions are added up to produce three raw scores. These raw scores equal the number you got right minus a fraction of the number you got wrong. These scores are converted into scaled scores, with 200 as the lowest score and 800 the highest. The three scaled scores are added together to produce your total score of 600–2400, as follows:

Section	Scaled Score Range	Sample Score
Writing	200–800	650
Math	200–800	710
Critical Reading	200–800	620
	Total: 600–2400	Total: 1980

GROUND RULES

These are SAT rules you can use to your advantage. Knowing these rules will keep you from wasting precious time and from committing minor errors that result in serious penalties.

- You are NOT allowed to jump back and forth between sections.
- You are NOT allowed to return to earlier sections to change answers.
- You are NOT allowed to spend more than the allotted time on any section.
- You CAN move around within a section.
- You CAN flip through your section at the beginning to see what types of questions are coming up.

SAT STRATEGIES

You Don't Have to Answer the Questions in Order

It's important to remember that you are allowed to skip around within each section of the SAT. Try not to dwell on any one question, even a hard one, until you have tried every question at least once. When you run into questions that look tough, circle them in your test booklet and skip them. Go back and try again after you have answered the easier ones. Remember, you don't get any extra points for answering hard questions.

There's another benefit for coming back to hard questions later. On a second look, troublesome questions can turn out to be simple. By answering some easier questions first, you can come back to a harder question with a fresh eye, a fresh perspective, and more confidence.

Keep Track of Time

Be careful at the end of a section when time may be running out. You don't want to have your answers in the test booklet and not be able to transfer them to your answer grid because you have run out of time. If it gets down to the wire, and you still have a few questions left, it would be a good idea to start transferring your answers one by one to ensure that every question you answered earns credit.

The Directions Never Change

One of the easiest things you can do to help your performance on the SAT is to understand the directions before taking the test. Because the directions are always exactly the same, there's no reason to waste your time reading them on the day of the test. On test day, eight sets of directions could take you eight minutes to read. Let's say you answer just one extra question right for every two minutes you save skipping the directions. That's four more questions—just from learning the directions in advance. That's big.

Be Prepared

Our advice is to not do any studying the night before the test. Instead, get together all of the following items to bring with you to the test:

A calculator with fresh batteries

A watch

A few No. 2 pencils (pencils with slightly dull points fill the ovals better)

Erasers

Photo ID card

Your admission ticket

A snack—there are breaks, and you'll probably get hungry

For more score-raising strategies, see "SAT Strategies" (Chapter two) of *The New SAT 2005 with CD-ROM*.

Chapter Two: **The Insider's Guide to the New SAT**

ESSENTIAL QUESTIONS AND ANSWERS

In this chapter you will find answers to the most pressing questions about the new exam.

What You Should Know About the Test Changes

Why are the tests changing?

The test makers are changing the SAT to make it more reflective of high school curriculum and more predictive of college success. The addition of the Writing section and the changes to the Math and Critical Reading sections should provide schools with a more complete picture of your preparedness for college-level work.

Why are these changes important?

The new test is longer, more difficult, and will require more in-depth preparation to achieve a high score. Knowing and understanding what's expected of you is half the battle.

Will the new test be harder?

Yes. The new Writing section will test your knowledge of grammar and usage and will require you to write an essay in 25 minutes. The new Math section will include advanced algebra. The test is longer so it will require more stamina.

How will the new Writing section be scored?

The essay will account for one-third of the Writing section's 800 total points. You will receive a raw score on the multiple-choice grammar and a 1–6-point score on the essay. These scores will be converted into a 200–800 scaled score.

How will the essay be graded?

Essay graders hired by the test makers will assign your essay a score of 1 to 6. Your essay will be graded by two readers. If the essay readers' scores differ by more than two points, the essay will be graded by a third reader. The graders will review many essays in a short period of time, so adherence to the graders' guidelines is essential.

What are the most important methods that will help me succeed on the new SAT?

It's critical to prepare thoroughly for the new exam. It's important to simulate test-like conditions when you complete practice questions in this book. Set aside 3 hours and 45 minutes of uninterrupted time so you can complete the entire exam in one sitting. Also, try taking your exam in an unfamiliar location. You won't take the real SAT in your bedroom, so it's probably not the best place to simulate testing conditions. By doing these things, you can see what it will be like on test day. This will also help you with time management during the test. Remember, the new SAT is longer, so pacing yourself will be critical on test day.

What else can I do to prepare for the new SAT?

Critical Reading: Because critical reading will be more important than ever on the new SAT, you should continue to develop the habit of reading as much as you can—for school as well as for pleasure.

Math: You should know that you get a double payoff when you do your math homework: You meet school requirements while getting a leg up on SAT preparation.

Writing: Try to listen to the everyday speech of different people— television sportscasters, radio DJs, and so on—and identify their mistakes of grammar or usage. A fun at-home exercise might be to start a "grammar-jar" to which household members contribute a quarter every time they're caught in a grammar mistake. Everyone makes missteps in speaking; training oneself to notice such errors can be a great way of preparing for the SAT. Also, try to spend a few minutes each day writing in a journal. This will get you into the habit of gathering your thoughts and placing them on paper—an important skill for the essay component of the exam.

THE MILLION-DOLLAR QUESTION—WHICH TEST SHOULD I TAKE?

Class of 2005

The class of 2005 will not be affected by the test changes. To meet your college application deadlines, you will need to take the current version of the SAT.

Class of 2006

The class of 2006 is presented with some unique opportunities surrounding the test changes. You will have the option of taking the current test, the new test, or both. How do you know which option is right for you? There are three simple questions that you need to ask:

1. Which test best addresses my skill set?

Consider the following: Are you a math whiz? Do you have strong grammar and writing skills? Is it easy for you to organize your thoughts quickly? Do you have strong reading comprehension skills? Advanced math, grammar, usage, and style questions and an essay will all appear on the new SAT. If these are areas of strength for you, this is the test that will best showcase your talents. Do you count a strong vocabulary among your intellectual assets? Do you excel at abstract questions like analogies and quantitative comparisons? Do you struggle with writing under timed conditions? Are you not always sure where to put the comma or which pronoun to use? If vocabulary and reasoning skills are your strong suit, and grammar, writing, and advanced math are not, you should make sure to take the current SAT before it changes.

2. Which exams do my target schools require?

Kaplan surveyed most of the top schools and found that of the schools that have formed a policy regarding the changing SAT, more than 80% will accept a combination of scores from both the current and new tests. To see a list of schools and their policies regarding SAT scores, see the following page.

3. Does it benefit me to take both exams?

In all likelihood, yes. In submitting standardized test scores, your goal is to put your best foot forward. Many of the schools that will accept scores from both exams have also said that they will consider the highest section score. This is a great opportunity to play to your strengths and show colleges what you can do.

Class of 2007

Like the class of 2005, the class of 2007 will not be affected by the test changes. If you're in the class of 2007, by the time you take the SAT, what is now the "new" test will be the only test available. Most colleges will not consider scores from the earlier version of the SAT for the class of 2007.

For students who will take both versions of the SAT, we have included the following timeline.

A Timeline for the Class of 2006

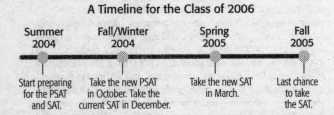

Summer 2004	Fall/Winter 2004	Spring 2005	Fall 2005
Start preparing for the PSAT and SAT.	Take the new PSAT in October. Take the current SAT in December.	Take the new SAT in March.	Last chance to take the SAT.

WHICH TEST DO COLLEGES WANT?

The class of 2006 is in the unique position to take both versions of the test. Kaplan Test Prep and Admissions surveyed college admissions officers at the top 500 colleges and universities nationwide to see which version of the SAT they want. As noted on the previous page, of the schools with policies regarding the two versions of the test, more than 80% of them said they will consider scores from both the current and new SATs. Many schools also indicated that they will take the highest Verbal and Math section scores that you submit.

Many schools have said they will accept scores from both the new and current test. Here is a select list. As schools formalize their policies and more information becomes available, it will be posted on www.kaptest.com/college.

Schools Accepting Both Current and New Test Scores

SCHOOL	STATE
Albion College	MI
Alcorn State University	MS
Auburn University	AL
Augustana College	IL
Augustana College	SD
Azusa Pacific University	CA
Belmont University	TN
Beloit College	WI
Centre College	KY
Champlain College	VT
City University of New York, Queens College	NY
Coker College	SC
College of Charleston	SC
College of New Jersey	NJ
College of William and Mary	VA
College of Wooster	OH
Colorado School of Mines	CO
Columbia University, Foundation School of Engineering and Applied Science	NY

Columbia University/Columbia College	NY
Concord College	WV
Concordia College	NY
Dartmouth College	NH
Emory University	GA
Fisk University	TN
Florida State University	FL
Fordham University	NY
Georgetown College	KY
Gettysburg College	PA
Grinnell College	IA
Hamilton College	NY
Hamline University	MN
Harding University	AR
Harvard University/Harvard College	MA
Harvey Mudd College	CA
Hobart and William Smith Colleges	NY
Hope College	MI
Illinois Wesleyan University	IL
Indiana University, Bloomington	IN
Johns Hopkins University	MD
Kenyon College	OH
Lewis and Clark College	OR
Lycoming College	PA
Macalester College	MN
Massachusetts Institute of Technology	MA
Merrimack College	MA
Millersville University of Pennsylvania	PA
Milwaukee School of Engineering	WI
Muhlenberg College	PA
Nazareth College of Rochester	NY
North Dakota State University	ND
Ohio State University	OH

Ohio Wesleyan University	OH
Oklahoma State University	OK
Oral Roberts University	OK
Oregon State University	OR
Pacific Union College	CA
Point Loma Nazarene University	CA
Polytechnic University	NY
Reed College	OR
Rice University	TX
Roberts Wesleyan College	NY
Rochester Institute of Technology	NY
Rose-Hulman Institute of Technology	IN
Rutgers, the State University of New Jersey– New Brunswick region	NJ
Saint Norbert College	WI
Saint Olaf College	MN
Saint Vincent College	PA
Southwest Texas State University	TX
Stanford University	CA
State University of New York, College at Geneseo	NY
State University of New York, Stony Brook	NY
Tennessee State University	TN
Trinity International University	IL
Truman State University	MO
United States Merchant Marine Academy	NY
United States Military Academy, West Point	NY
University of Hawaii, Manoa	HI
University of Iowa	IA
University of Massachusetts, Boston	MA
University of Mississippi	MS
University of New Mexico	NM
University of Northern Colorado	CO
University of Oklahoma	OK

University of Rhode Island	RI
University of Richmond	VA
University of South Carolina, Columbia	SC
University of Tennessee	TN
University of the Pacific	CA
University of Vermont	VT
University of Wisconsin, Eau Claire	WI
University of Wisconsin, La Crosse	WI
University of Wisconsin, Superior	WI
Ursinus College	PA
Virginia Military Institute	VA
Wartburg College	IA
Washington and Jefferson College	PA
Washington and Lee University	VA
Washington University in St. Louis	MO
Webb Institute	NY
Wells College	NY
Western Maryland College	MD
Western Washington University	WA
Westminster College	MO
Westmont College	CA
Whitman College	WA
Wofford College	SC
Yale University	CT

Source: Kaplan Test Prep and Admissions

Based on phone confirmations from senior admissions officials at more than 200 of the top 500 colleges and universities nationwide. Top 500 schools list compiled from *U.S. News and World Report's Ultimate College Directory*, 2004 Edition and *Barron's Profiles of American Colleges*, 25th Edition. Sampling error +/−7%.

For updates, visit www.kaptest.com/college.

Chapter Three: **The New SAT Essay**

INTRODUCTION TO THE SAT ESSAY

The Writing section is completely new on the SAT 2005, so it's important to know how it's set up and scored. There is only one Writing section on the SAT, but that section is broken up into two parts. The first part is a student-produced essay—that's what this chapter is all about. The essay is worth one-third of your total Writing score. The second part contains multiple-choice questions, which we will discuss in the next chapter. On test day, you will have 25 minutes to complete the essay portion of this section.

THE ESSAY

On the new SAT essay section, you will be asked to read a prompt and write an essay using information from your own experience or knowledge to support your position. Your essay should be persuasive. Graders will score the essays on a scale from 1 to 6 (6 being the highest score); more about what these numbers mean later. There are three important factors that graders consider when scoring your essay: length (essays should be between 300–400 words), content, and neatness.

KEY ASPECTS OF THE ESSAY SECTION

When writing your essay, keep the following important points in mind:

- Do not use oversized handwriting. You will receive only two pages (42 lines) on which to write your essay, and if you run out of space, you will not get more.

- Your handwriting must be neat and legible. Graders have only a short amount of time to read each essay, and if your handwriting is messy and hard to follow, they may conclude that the content itself is, too.

- Be careful to answer the question asked. If you write about a topic other than the one given, you will not receive any points.

- When writing your essay, stay away from offensive language or clichés. Also, remember your audience, and tailor your persuasive argument toward it.

- If you finish your essay early, you can move on to the multiple-choice section right away.

WRAPPING IT UP

Try this practice essay to get an idea of what it will be like on test day. Set aside 25 minutes to write your essay. When you are finished, review the scoring guide and sample essays. By completing this practice exercise, you'll be able to recognize your strengths and weaknesses, and you'll know exactly where to go for more help.

SAT ESSAY WRITING PRACTICE

Directions: Consider carefully the following statement and the assignment below it.

"Creativity is allowing yourself to make mistakes.
Art is knowing which ones to keep."

—Scott Adams

Assignment: What is your view of the idea that mistakes are necessary for creativity? Support your position by discussing an example (or examples) from literature, science and technology, the arts, current events, or your own experience or observation.

_____

_____

_____

_____

_____

_____

_____

_____

_____

_____

_____

_____

_____

_____

_____

_____

_____

_____

_____

_____

_____

_____

_____

_____

_____

_____

_____

_____

_____

_____

_____

_____

_____

_____

_____

_____

_____

_____

_____

_____

_____

_____

_____

_____

_____

SAMPLE SCORING GUIDE AND ESSAYS

SAT Essay Scoring Guide

Here are a few of the qualities of a 6, 5, and 4 essay.

Score 6

Addresses the topic in depth

Shows variety in syntax and a range of vocabulary

Shows insight

Supports details with specific examples

Shows logical thought and organization

Avoids major errors in word use that lead to unclear writing

Score 5

Addresses the topic in depth

Supports details with specific examples

Shows logical thought and organization

Avoids major errors in word use that lead to unclear writing

Score 4

Addresses the topic

Supports details with examples

Shows logical thought and organization

Avoids major errors in word use that lead to unclear writing

GET A SECOND OPINION

Since you are probably not the best judge of your own work, ask at least two trusted friends or teachers to read your practice essay. Ask them what score (1–6) they honestly believe you should earn. Take their constructive criticisms and apply them to your next practice essay.

Sample Essay

Here are sample essays based on the prompt from the practice. There is a 4 essay and a 6 essay. Before reading the 6 essay, think of what you could do to the 4, the adequate essay, to make it shine as a 6.

4 Essay

The statement says that creativity is the result of mistakes. Mistakes are infortuitous, unexpected and not always happy events, but like most art, they are usually original. But are they art? Usually art is something done on purpose and intentionally. Beethoven, a classical musician, was once considered a revolutionary and his music was considered out-of-bounds. But are originality and creativity the same as a mistake? Does the artistic process need mistakes?

Beethoven's originality was due to egregious study and work, and was not based on random mistakes. Beethoven worked constantly on his work, changing it over and over again until he was satisfied. Beethoven first made a name for himself as a pianist rather than as a composer. His dramatic improvisations and virtuoso technique made an impression in society, but not before he had carefully studied Haydn, Mozart, C.P.E. Bach and Clementi. The early work was original and highly creative, but it was based on work and practice, not trial and error, even when it was spontaneous.

In the Eroica, Symphony #3, Beethoven introduced many creative elements that were not understood by audiences at first. These artistic creations, although called mistakes by some, were not random. In this middle period more than ever, he would work constantly on a musical idea, writing it over and over again before he called it finished.

Till the end of his life, he worked this way, burdened by his deafness and many other problems.

Mistakes tend to just happen, but great art takes work and sometimes a lot of pain and suffering as Beethoven's case shows. Creativity is usually the result of training and work, not mistakes, which anyone could make. Mistaking creativity for a mistake can be a mistake.

This essay is a 4 because it addresses the prompt in a reasonably organized way with some lapses in form and style. Once you get past the awkward introduction, real ideas are presented, and an example is chosen and developed. Together, these are presented well enough to make the grade to a decent score.

6 Essay

Mistakes are unexpected and not always happy events. Like art, they can be original. However, art is something done intentionally. Beethoven, a classical musician, was once considered a revolutionary and his music, original and creative, was considered out-of-bounds. But was his originality and creativity the result of mistakes? Beethoven's case seems to demonstrate that they are the result of study, practice, and careful planning.

Beethoven worked constantly on his compositions, changing them relentlessly until he was satisfied. Beethoven first made a name for himself as a pianist rather than as a composer. His dramatic improvisations and virtuoso technique made a powerful impression in society. These performances seemed freewheeling, and were spur-of-the moment with many original themes, but Beethoven did not come to these performances unprepared. Before becoming known as a master improvisor, Beethoven carefully studied Haydn, Mozart, C.P.E. Bach and Clementi. The early work was original and highly creative, but it was based on practice and planning, not trial and error, even when it was spontaneous

In the Eroica, Symphony #3, Beethoven introduced many creative elements that were not understood by audiences at first. These artistic creations, called mistakes by some, were not random. In this middle period, he would work constantly on a musical idea, transforming it hundreds of times before he called it finished. Till the end of his life, he worked this way. Even though he was burdened by his deafness and many other problems, Beethoven continued composing, always changing and reworking his music, looking for perfection in his art.

As most of us well know, mistakes tend to just happen, but great art takes work. Creativity is usually the result of training and practice, not a lucky break or fortuitous mistake. Anyone can make a mistake; not everyone can write a symphony.

Could you see the difference between the 4 and 6 essays? You can easily achieve a 6 essay if you are well prepared and use your time effectively. Kaplan has developed several ace strategies for writing a great essay on test day.

To be prepared for the SAT Essay you need a thorough understanding of the assignment. Because you only have 25 minutes to complete your essay, you also have to know how to budget your time, and how best to organize your essay. You can find all of this information, as well as details about scoring in *The New SAT Writing Workbook*. This book also provides targeted strategies and comprehensive practice for scoring higher on the Writing section.

Chapter Four: **The New SAT Writing Section**

INTRODUCTION TO SAT WRITING

As we discussed in the previous chapter, there are two parts to the Writing section. The second part contains multiple-choice questions in three different forms, and you will have 35 minutes to complete them. You should take these questions seriously, because they are worth two-thirds of your total Writing score and nearly 20% of your overall SAT score. To help boost your confidence, we will give you an overview of the three question types that appear on the multiple-choice section.

MULTIPLE-CHOICE QUESTIONS

There are three types of multiple-choice questions on the new SAT Writing section.

Usage Questions

These ask you to identify, but not correct, a possible error in a sentence.

Sentence Correction Questions

These ask you to identify a possible error in a sentence and choose the best correction. You will always have the option to keep the original sentence.

Paragraph Correction Questions

These ask you to identify the best ways to organize, revise, replace, or combine words or sentences from a rough draft of an essay.

WRAPPING IT UP

Now you're ready to start practicing. We're giving you 16 questions covering each multiple-choice question type. Answer the multiple-choice questions first and then review the answer explanations. By completing this practice set, you'll be able to recognize your strengths and weaknesses, and you'll know exactly where to go for more help.

SAT WRITING PRACTICE SET

Usage Questions

1. Tolstoy's grasp of detail <u>enabled him to create</u>
                                                    (A)

   novels that <u>arose from</u> <u>and reflected</u> the complexity
                        (B)   (C)

   of events that Russians <u>have endured</u>. <u>No error</u>
                                        (D)   (E)

2. This month, the Five and Dime Store <u>lowered</u>
                                                                (A)

   prices as a way <u>at attracting</u> a larger number
                            (B)

   <u>of customers</u> during the <u>back to school season</u>.
       (C)   (D)

   <u>No error</u>
       (E)

3. The soldier, after his successful <u>infiltration</u> into
                                      (A)

   enemy territory, <u>went about</u> <u>heavy camouflaged</u>
                         (B)   (C)

   and was reachable by <u>only a handful</u> of his
                              (D)

   comrades. <u>No error</u>
               (E)

4. In the mid-twentieth century, costuming <u>for</u> story
                                            (A)

   ballets and short dances <u>were</u> greatly improved <u>by</u>
                             (B)   (C)

   the <u>designs of</u> the New York City Ballet's Karinska.
        (D)

   <u>No error</u>
     (E)

5. With the aid of an enormous truck, the

   <u>electric company</u> employee <u>rose</u> the new electric
        (A)   (B)

   pole <u>on the</u> street corner <u>across from</u> the school.
         (C)   (D)

   <u>No error</u>
     (E)

Sentence Correction Questions

6. The devastating impact of <u>many diseases, often unchecked in developing nations because</u> education and information are difficult to spread.

   (A) many diseases, often unchecked in developing nations because

   (B) many diseases is often unchecked in developing nations where

   (C) many diseases is often unchecked in developing nations and

   (D) many diseases, often unchecked in developing nations when

   (E) many diseases, often unchecked in developing nations and

7. As freshman year continues, the balance between academics and socializing <u>become more important, challenging, and it can frighten first-year students</u>.

   (A) become more important, challenging, and it can frighten first-year students

   (B) becomes important, challenging and frightening

   (C) when it becomes important, challenging, and frightening

   (D) becoming important, challenging and frightening to first year students

   (E) becomes important, challenging and it can frighten one

8. <u>Due to its timely subject matter</u>, Arthur Miller's latest play is earning stellar reviews.

    (A) Due to its timely subject matter

    (B) The subject matter is timely

    (C) Due to the subject matter's timeliness

    (D) The subject matter of it being timely

    (E) The subject matter having been timely

9. <u>Ronaldo is a world-class soccer player, he is famous for scoring goals in the World Cup, and he</u> will play for Brazil in the next international match.

    (A) Ronaldo is a world-class soccer player, he is famous for scoring goals in the World Cup, and he

    (B) Ronaldo is a world-class soccer player who is famous for scoring goals in the World Cup and

    (C) Ronaldo, a world-class soccer player whose goal scoring in the World Cup being famous,

    (D) Ronaldo, a world-class soccer player famous for his goal scoring in the World Cup,

    (E) Ronaldo, a world-class soccer player, the goal scoring in the World Cup of which is famous

10. Lying on Ireland's southwest shore, <u>the history of Kinsale is a prime example of</u> fierce fighting between the Irish and the English.

    (A) the history of Kinsale is a prime example of

    (B) the history of Kinsale is primarily an example of

    (C) the history of Kinsale comes from

    (D) Kinsale's history comes from

    (E) Kinsale is a prime historical example of

11. Learning two languages is common among French students, the majority <u>of them need</u> proficiency in English to embark on business careers.

(A) of them need

(B) of them are needing

(C) which need

(D) of whom need

(E) need

Paragraph Correction Questions

Questions 12–16 are based on the following passage.

(1) *One of the most important achievements after the American Revolution was the creation of the presidential office.* (2) *This was difficult because they feared popular leadership.* (3) *In the Founding Fathers' view, it was dangerous for the President to gain power from popularity.*

(4) *The Founders believed in the ignorance of the populace.* (5) *The office of the President needed to be independent of the popular will and the "common man."*

(6) *George Washington was a perfect example.* (7) *Just exactly as the Founders had always wished for, Washington's heroics and also regal bearing put him way up high on a pedestal.* (8) *However, some of America's most famous presidents did not follow the Founders' ideals.* (9) *Andrew Jackson (nicknamed "Old Hickory") identified himself as a "common man" and used his popularity as a military hero to win the presidential election.* (10) *In other words, he makes the presidency what it is today: a popularity contest.*

(11) *Fourteen years later, Abraham Lincoln was virtually everything the Founders had not wanted in a leader.* (12) *He did not stand above popular opinion.* (13) *He courted public favor as "Honest Abe."* (14) *He had humble roots, a fact that he emphasized to gain public favor.* (15) *The Founders would have hated this.* (16) *But many people think that Lincoln was one of our best Presidents.* (17) *This suggests maybe they were wrong.*

12. Which of the following best replaces the word *they* in sentence 2?

    (A) the revolutionaries
    (B) the complications
    (C) the Founding Fathers
    (D) the Presidents
    (E) the populace

13. In context, which of the following words are the most logical to insert at the beginning of sentence 5?

    (A) I have found that
    (B) On the other hand
    (C) And yet, for him
    (D) To them,
    (E) Resulting in,

14. In context, which is the best version of sentence 7?

    (A) (As it is now)

    (B) George Washington is regal and bearing and heroic and
        they wanted to place him on a pedestal.

    (C) As the Founders had always wished, the pedestal was
        there for Washington's regal bearing and heroics.

    (D) As the Founders wished, Washington's heroics and regal
        bearing put him on a pedestal.

    (E) As the Founders wished, Washington's heroics and regal
        bearing made it possible for him to be put way up
        high on a pedestal.

15. In context, which of the following revisions is necessary in
    sentence 10?

    (A) Replace *he* with *Jackson*

    (B) Replace *the presidency* with *the President*

    (C) Replace *it is* with *it was*

    (D) Replace *makes* with *had made*

    (E) Replace *makes* with *made*

16. In context, which is the best way to combine sentences 16 and 17 (reproduced below)?

    But many people think that Lincoln was one of our best Presidents. This suggests maybe they were wrong.

    (A) They were wrong, many people suggested, thinking that Lincoln was one of our best Presidents.

    (B) Suggesting that they were wrong, many people think that Lincoln was one of our best Presidents.

    (C) But many people think that Lincoln was one of our best presidents, which suggests that maybe the Founders were wrong.

    (D) Furthermore, many people think that Lincoln was one of our best Presidents, suggesting that maybe the Founders were wrong.

    (E) Yet, maybe the Founders were wrong, many people think that Lincoln was one of our best Presidents.

ANSWERS AND EXPLANATIONS

1. E

Choice (E) is correct just as many times as the other answer choices are. In this sentence, there is no error. All of the verbs listed are idiomatically correct and in the appropriate tense.

2. B

Prepositions are commonly tested on the SAT, so you should learn about the most commonly tested prepositional phrases. The sentence contains many prepositions, so look to see if they are used appropriately. *At attracting* is idiomatically incorrect. The correct phrase is *as a way to attract*. *Lowered* is appropriate, because it refers to something that happened in the past. *Of customers* uses the appropriate preposition. *Back to school season* is an appropriate idiomatic expression.

3. C

The word *heavy* is an adjective, which can modify only nouns or pronouns, but here it modifies the participle *camouflaged*. We need an adverb and (C) should read *heavily camouflaged*. *Infiltration* is a correct noun. *Went about* and *only a handful* are standard written English.

4. B

The phrase *story ballets and short dances* lies in between the subject and verb, making it more difficult to see the agreement problem. The subject of the sentence is the singular noun *costuming* and so the verb *were* (B) should be changed to the singular *was*.

5. B

Good diction means learning to be sensitive to subtle distinctions between similar words. The correct word is *raised* (which means put up or lifted and usually has a direct object, as in the employee *raised* the pole). *Rose* (B) is the past tense of *rise* (which means stand up or go up), which doesn't fit. The adjective phrase *electric company* correctly describes the employee. The prepositions *on* and *from* are correctly used in (C) and (D).

6. B

This sentence is a fragment; there is no verb in an independent clause. The verb *are* is in the second clause, which is made subordinate by the conjunction *because*. (B) and (C) add the word *is* in the independent clause and are complete sentences. Only (B) keeps the sentence's original meaning. (C) loses the causal relationship between the two clauses. (D) and (E) don't correct the original problem—they are still fragments.

7. B

There are three major problems in this sentence. First, when you see a pronoun such as *it*, check whether the sentence clearly shows to what the pronoun refers. Second, check for parallelism in a series (*important, challenging, and it can frighten*...). Third, check subject/verb agreement. The pronoun *it* has no clear antecedent and *it can frighten first-year students* is not parallel to the first two items *important* and *challenging*. Also, the plural verb *become* does not agree with the singular noun *balance*. Only (B) corrects all of those problems and removes the redundant *first-year students*. (C) corrects the problems but introduces *when*, which is incorrect. (D) is a fragment, replacing *become* with *becoming*. (E) only addresses the subject/verb agreement problem.

8. A

Approximately 20% of Sentence Correction questions have no errors. Knowing this could earn you valuable points on the SAT Writing section. The sentence concisely establishes a cause in its first half, and a logical result in its second half. (B) creates two separate sentences with no clear relationship. (C) is grammatically correct, but much more awkward than the original sentence. (D) is even more awkward. (E) introduces the perfect tense without any reason.

9. D

This sentence is long and rambling—a sentence type that the SAT
frowns on. Look for the relationship among the several ideas. What is
subordinate? What is modifying or causal? The main action is that
Ronaldo will play for Brazil in the next international match. Everything
else provides information about Ronaldo. (D) puts all the information
in the proper place. It introduces Ronaldo, gives some description,
and then states that he will play for Brazil. (B) clarifies that the first
two ideas are descriptions of Ronaldo, but does not make these
descriptions subordinate to his playing for Brazil. (C) makes the first
half of the sentence a dependent clause. (E) introduces *of which* and
it confuses the meaning of the sentence.

10. E

The SAT regularly tests your ability to recognize and correct misplaced
modifiers. On this question type, when there is an introductory
phrase, check to see if it is modified correctly. Kinsale lies on Ireland's
southwest shore. The *history of Kinsale* does not. (E) rearranges the
sentence to make this clear. (B) and (C) don't address the principle
problem. (D) corrects the problem but is awkward and has the open-
ing phrase modifying a possessive (*Kinsale's* instead of *Kinsale*).

11. D

The entire sentence is a run-on with a comma splice, as neither clause
is subordinate to the other. How can we make the second clause subordinate? (D) does the trick. It uses the objective form *whom* to create
a clause that correctly modifies *French students*. (B) is still a run-on
and only substitutes *are serving* for the simple present used in the
original sentence. (C) uses *which* to refer to people instead of *whom*.
(E) is also still a run-on. An important strategy for this question type is
not to focus only on the words that are underlined.

12. C

There is no plural noun before *they* so we must read further.
Sentence 3 states that the Founding Fathers considered it *dangerous*
for the President to gain power from popularity. Therefore, it is the
Founding Fathers who *feared popular leadership*, and (C) is correct.
(A) is incorrect; revolutionaries are never mentioned, just the
Revolution itself. (B) is illogical; complications cannot fear anything.
(D) and (E) pick up the wrong words from sentence 3.

13. D

Your score will improve on multiple-choice questions and on the essay if you understand how to organize your writing. Adding a phrase to the beginning of sentence 5 will probably set up its relationship to sentence 4. Sentence 5 makes a conclusion based on the Founders' idea in sentence 4. (D) refers to the Founders and shows that sentence 5 definitely follows from sentence 4. (A) uses the first person, although the author never refers to herself in the passage. (B) and (C) incorrectly set up a contrast between sentences 5 and 4. (C) also adds the pronoun *him*, which doesn't clearly refer to anyone. (E) creates a sentence fragment.

14. D

As it is written, sentence 7 is wordy and unclear, which makes (A) incorrect. Choice (B) changes the meaning of Washington's qualities from *regal bearing* to *regal and bearing*. Choice (C) does not convey the same information as the original sentence intended. Choice (E), although more clear, is too wordy and uses the passive voice. Only choice (D) maintains the meaning of the original sentence, and presents the information in a clear and concise manner. On the SAT Writing section, you will need to recognize clear and concise writing in the multiple-choice questions, and produce clear and concise writing on the essay.

15. E

This sentence confuses tenses. Andrew Jackson acted in the past to make the presidency what it is in the present. (E) correctly puts *makes* in the past tense. (A) is incorrect because *he* is not ambiguous; *he* clearly refers to Andrew Jackson. (B) is illogical; the President isn't a popularity contest, the presidency is. (C) and (D) make the wrong tense change. (C) puts what is happening in the present into the past tense. (D) changes to the past perfect tense, which would work only if a later action by Jackson was mentioned.

16. C

As written, the sentence states that *many people* may have been wrong. But the author's point is that *the Founders* may have been wrong. (C) corrects that problem and substitutes *the Founders* for the ambiguous pronoun *they*. (A) and (B) change the meaning to say that the people actively suggested that the Founders were wrong. (D) uses the wrong transition word; it should be a word that indicates contrasts with sentence 15. (E) is a run-on sentence with a comma splice.

FOR MORE HELP...

Each multiple-choice question in this practice set deals primarily with one topic relating to grammar or writing. Knowing which topics give you the most trouble will help you focus on exactly what to study. Use the following table to find out where you can get even more practice with these skills. Kaplan's *The NEW SAT Writing Workbook* is a great resource for additional writing practice.

Question Number	Topic	Chapter	Chapter Topic
1	No Error	6	Usage Questions
2	Idioms	6	Usage Questions
3	Adjectives and Adverbs	6	Usage Questions
4	Subject/Verb Agreement	6	Usage Questions
5	Diction/Word Choice	6	Usage Questions
6	Sentence Fragments	7	Sentence Correction Questions
7	Wordiness/Redundancy	7	Sentence Correction Questions
8	No Error	7	Sentence Correction Questions

Question Number	Topic	Chapter	Chapter Topic
9	Dependent and Independent Clauses	7	Sentence Correction Questions
10	Misplaced Modifiers	7	Sentence Correction Questions
11	Run-On sentences	7	Sentence Correction Questions
12	Word Choice	8	Paragraph Correction Questions
13	Introductory Phrases	8	Paragraph Correction Questions
14	Clarity	8	Paragraph Correction Questions
15	Grammar	8	Paragraph Correction Questions
16	Combining Sentences	8	Paragraph Correction Questions

Do you know the multiple-choice writing questions are worth two-thirds of your entire SAT Writing score? For this reason, your knowledge of grammar and usage are critical. For a comprehensive review of grammar skills and multiple-choice strategies, check out Kaplan's *The New SAT 2005 with CD-ROM*. This comprehensive guide includes critical information about the test and the best ways to raise your score on test day.

Chapter Five: **The New SAT Critical Reading Section**

INTRODUCTION TO SAT CRITICAL READING

The Critical Reading section of the SAT used to be called the Verbal section. Although the format has not changed drastically, it is important that you know how the new section is set up. There are three Critical Reading sections on the exam that will include both Sentence Completion questions and Reading Comprehension questions. You will have 25 minutes for the first two sections and 20 minutes for the last section. Knowing what to expect from each question type will give you the extra edge that you need.

SENTENCE COMPLETION QUESTIONS

This question type tests your ability to see how the parts of a sentence relate. In other words, they test your reading and vocabulary skills. About half the questions have one word missing from the sentence; the rest have two words missing.

Sentence Completion questions are arranged in order of difficulty. Keeping this in mind can help you maximize your time and your score on these questions.

READING COMPREHENSION QUESTIONS

There are two types of passages in the Critical Reading sections: short passages (approximately 100 words) and long passages (approximately 450–800 words). There are also four types of questions: Main Idea questions, Detail questions, Vocabulary-in-Context questions, and Inference questions.

Unlike Sentence Completion questions, Reading Comprehension questions are *not* arranged by order of difficulty. If you find yourself spending too much time on a question, you should skip it and come back to it later.

PAIRED PASSAGES

The Reading Comprehension sections will also include some paired passages, or two passages on a related topic. The questions that will follow these paired passages will be a little different from those that follow single passages. For example, you may be asked to compare or contrast the two passages.

WRAPPING IT UP

Now you're ready to start practicing. We're giving you a long passage and a short passage as well as 16 questions covering each question type. Practice solving these questions and review the answers and explanations found at the end of this chapter. By completing these practice questions, you'll be able to recognize your strengths and weaknesses, and you'll know where to find the extra help you need.

HOT TOPICS

Reading passages on the SAT may be drawn from the humanities, social sciences, natural sciences, or fiction. You will not need to have any previous knowledge about a topic. Everything you need to know will be right there in front of you.

SAT CRITICAL READING PRACTICE SET

1. The lecturer's frustration was only - - - - by the audience's
   - - - - to talk during her presentation.
   (A) compounded .. propensity
   (B) alleviated .. invitation
   (C) soothed .. authorization
   (D) increased .. inability
   (E) supplanted .. desire

2. The journalist's claim of - - - - is belied by her record of
   campaign fund contributions to only one party's candidates.
   (A) innocence
   (B) corruption
   (C) impartiality
   (D) affluence
   (E) loyalty

3. Emphysema, a chronic lung disease, can occur in either a
   localized or - - - - form.
   (A) a contained
   (B) an acute
   (C) a restricted
   (D) a diffuse
   (E) a fatal

4. Clint Eastwood made his reputation playing tough, - - - - characters, notable for their expressive yet - - - - speech.

   (A) laconic . . pithy
   (B) narcissistic . . obtuse
   (C) pragmatic . . enthusiastic
   (D) esoteric . . trite
   (E) monotonous . . interesting

5. The defendant was - - - - even though he presented evidence that proved he was nowhere near the scene of the crime.

   (A) abandoned
   (B) indicted
   (C) exculpated
   (D) exhumed
   (E) rescinded

6. She would never have believed that her article was so - - - - were it not for the - - - - of correspondence which followed its publication.

   (A) interesting . . dearth
   (B) inflammatory . . lack
   (C) controversial . . spate
   (D) commonplace . . influx
   (E) insignificant . . volume

7. The inflated tone with which some art historians narrate exhibitions would make one think that to attain a legitimate appreciation of art, one is required not only to devote years to its study, but also to possess the ability to offer - - - - interpretations of artistic pieces.

(A) subversive

(B) grandiloquent

(C) intractable

(D) clairvoyant

(E) immutable

8. Some English scholars believe that students tend to have greater difficulty understanding Shakespeare than they do other authors because his works become - - - - on the printed page; it is in their performance that their meaning - - - -.

(A) opaque . . emerges

(B) obtuse . . dispels

(C) muddled . . tapers

(D) evident . . emanates

(E) overwrought . . ensues

Questions 9–14 are based on the following passage.

The following passage is excerpted from a major scientific journal.

The transformer is an essential component of modern electric power systems. Simply put, it can convert electricity with a low current and a high voltage into electricity with a high current and low voltage (and vice versa) with
5   almost no loss of energy. The conversion is important because electric power is transmitted most efficiently at high voltages but is best generated and used at low voltages. Were it not for transformers, the distance separating generators from consumers would have to be minimized,
10 many households and industries would require their own power stations, and electricity would be a much less practical form of energy.

In addition to its role in electric power systems, the transformer is an integral component of many things that
15 run on electricity. Desk lamps, battery chargers, toy trains, and television sets all rely on transformers to cut or boost voltage. In all its multiplicity of applications, the transformer can range from tiny assemblies the size of a pea to behemoths weighing 500 tons or more. The principles
20 that govern the function of electrical transformers are the same regardless of form or application.

The English physicist Michael Faraday discovered the basic action of the transformer during his pioneering investigations of electricity in 1831. Some fifty years later,
25 the advent of a practical transformer, containing all the essential elements of the modern instrument, revolutionized the infant electric lighting industry. By the turn of the century, alternating-current power systems had been universally adopted and the transformer had assumed a key
30 role in electrical transmission and distribution.

Yet the transformer's tale does not end in 1900. Today's transformers can handle 500 times the power and 15

times the voltage of their turn-of-the-century ancestors;
the weight per unit of power has dropped by a factor of
35 ten and efficiency typically exceeds 99 percent. These
advances reflect the marriage of theoretical inquiry and
engineering that first elucidated and then exploited the
phenomena governing transformer action.

Faraday's investigations were inspired by the Danish
40 physicist Hans Christian Oersted, who had shown in 1820
that an electric current flowing through a conducting
material creates a magnetic field around the conductor. At
the time, Oersted's discovery was considered remarkable,
since electricity and magnetism were thought to be sepa-
45 rate and unrelated forces. If an electric current could gen-
erate a magnetic field, it seemed likely that a magnetic
field could give rise to an electric current.

In 1831, Faraday demonstrated that in order for a magnetic field to induce a current in a conductor, the field
50 must be changing. Faraday caused the strength of the field
to fluctuate by making and breaking the electric circuit
generating the field; the same effect can be achieved with a
current whose direction alternates in time. This fascinat-
ing interaction of electricity and magnetism came to be
55 known as electromagnetic induction.

9. According to the passage, the first practical transformer was
   developed in
   (A) 1820
   (B) 1831
   (C) 1860
   (D) 1881
   (E) 1900

10. The passage suggests that advances in the efficiency of the transformer are
    (A) based solely on Faraday's discovery of electromagnetic induction
    (B) due to a combination of engineering and theoretical curiosity
    (C) continuing to occur at an ever accelerated pace
    (D) most likely at a peak that cannot be surpassed
    (E) found in transformers that weigh 500 tons or more

11. In line 29, *assumed* most nearly means
    (A) presupposed
    (B) understood
    (C) feigned
    (D) taken
    (E) borrowed

12. Which of the following is NOT true of transformers today as compared to the first transformers?
    (A) They comprise the same basic components.
    (B) They are lighter in weight.
    (C) They are many times more powerful.
    (D) They operate at a much lower voltage.
    (E) They are almost completely efficient.

13. According to the passage, one function of the transformer is to
    (A) convert electricity into the high voltages most useful for transmission
    (B) create the magnetic fields used in industry
    (C) minimize the distance between generators and consumers
    (D) protect electric power systems from energy loss
    (E) transform electrical energy into a magnetic field

14. Which of the following statements is best supported by the passage?
    (A) Faraday was the first to show how an electric current can induce a magnetic field.
    (B) Oersted was the first to utilize transformers in a practical application, by using them to power electric lights.
    (C) Faraday invented the first practical transformer.
    (D) Oersted coined the term electromagnetic induction.
    (E) Faraday demonstrated that when a magnetic field is changing, it can produce an electric current in a conducting material.

Questions 15–16 are based on the following passage.

The comedy of manners reached its height in mid-seventeenth century France and England. In France, the most outstanding playwright of the genre was Molière, whose comedies mocked the social pretensions and moral
5 hypocrisy of both the court circle and the middle class, while in England, Restoration dramatists such as William Wycherley and William Congreve took their cue from Molière. Cynical, witty, and epigrammatic by turns, Restoration plays were as popular under King Charles II
10 as the dramas of Shakespeare and his contemporaries had been nearly a century earlier. However, it was the foibles of society, rather than the fortunes of kings and heroes, that became their principal theme.

15. The author would most likely agree that

   (A) the plays of Shakespeare and his contemporaries focused largely on heroic and royal subjects

   (B) Molière was the most innovative of the Restoration dramatists

   (C) the comedy of manners was primarily popular both in France and in England, though for different reasons

   (D) the French court circle and middle class could be well described as both witty and cynical

   (E) Restoration plays are the finest examples of English drama

16. The phrase *took their cue from Molière* (lines 7–8) conveys that Restoration playwrights
    (A) hoped to achieve the same level of success as Molière
    (B) were influenced by Molière in their artistic aims
    (C) depended on Molière for thematic inspiration
    (D) likely studied with Molière to learn his techniques
    (E) modeled each of their plays on works by Molière

ANSWERS AND EXPLANATIONS

1. A

Solve the question by examining the question. In this sentence, a lecturer is frustrated by something her audience has done. This frustration was only - - - - by some connection between the audience and talking. It sounds like the lecturer was frustrated by her audience's desire or tendency to talk during her presentation. So, for the second blank, we want something like desire—choice (A) *propensity*, or tendency, and choice (E) *desire* could work. To choose between (A) and (E), look at the second blank. (E) is illogical, so (A) must be correct. In fact, it makes the most sense.

2. C

What claim would be belied or contradicted by a record of contributing to only one party? Choice (C) gets it with *impartiality*, or not favoring one side over the other.

3. D

To solve this question, you need to understand how to find clue words. In this sentence, the clue words are *either* and *or*. This offers a choice of two options which do not mean the same thing. If one of the options is a localized . . . form, the other has to be a [nonlocalized] form. So the correct answer will mean nonlocalized. Let's say you didn't know the word localized. You probably do know the word local. It means near you, in your area, and not all over the place. So, localized will have something to do with a limited space. (A) and (C) don't work. (D) *diffuse* means spread out, the opposite of localized, so it's correct.

4. A

The key to completing a sentence is to tie up loose ends without adding any new or unrelated information. The clue word *yet* should help you limit the choices up front. The second word will be something not usually associated with *expressive*. The first word will be one that goes well with *tough*. That lets you eliminate (C) and (E) based on their second blanks. That leaves (A), (B), and (D) for the first blank. Someone tough isn't necessarily (B) *narcissistic* or (D) *esoteric*. But he could very well be (A) *laconic*. The two words in (A), *laconic* and *pithy*, best fit our predictions.

5. B

The phrase *even though* indicates contrast. So, *even though* the prisoner presented evidence proving that he was nowhere near the scene of the crime, he was (B) *indicted*, or formally charged with committing the crime. To find the correct answer, you should always look at the preceding conjunctions and contrasting phrases.

6. C

It is clear that the content of the journalist's article either had no impact, in which case there was little or no response from the public, or it attracted a great deal of attention and was followed by a lot of correspondence. (C) is the correct answer. The author would never have thought her article was so *controversial* were it not for the *spate* of correspondence.

7. B

Your context clue in this sentence is *inflated tone*, so you should look for a word that describes an ability that would result in an inflated tone, such as bombastic. *Grandiloquent*, (B), matches our prediction. If you don't know the definition, you could break the word apart: *grand* = big, *loq* = talk. Of the wrong answer choices, *subversive* means corrupting; *intractable* means unyielding; *clairvoyant* means psychic; and *immutable* means unchanging, none of which matches our prediction.

8. A

You have two structural clues in this sentence: the word *because* and the use of a semicolon. Each indicates that the sentence will continue in one direction throughout. If students have difficulty understanding Shakespeare in English classes, you can assume that his works become harder to understand on the printed page, which is how students would be experiencing them. Meanwhile, in performance, their meaning would come forth. So, even though the sentence continues in one direction, the two words will contrast with each other: one meaning harder to see, and the other meaning easier to see. Regarding the first blank: Neither *evident* nor *overwrought* means difficult to understand, so rule out (D) and (E). Regarding the second blank: Neither *dispels* nor *tapers* contrasts with the first word in each set, making (B) and (C) incorrect. Try reading (A) into the sentence. To be *opaque* is to be difficult to understand, whereas *emerges* means comes forth, so (A) is correct.

9. D

The first question asks you to consider details from the passage. The passage says that Faraday *discovered the basic action of the transformer* in 1831 (lines 22–23). But note that it was not until 50 years later that a practical transformer was developed (lines 24–25). This means that the first practical transformer was developed in 1881.

10. B

This is an Inference question. To solve it you should refer to the fourth paragraph. The paragraph lists several advances in the transformer in lines 31–35. This list is followed by the statement that the *advances reflect the marriage of theoretical inquiry and engineering that first elucidated and then exploited the phenomena governing transformer action* (lines 36–38). This makes (B) the best answer.

11. D

This is a Vocabulary-in-Context question. Here's how to find out the meaning of *assumed*. Based on the sentence in which it is found, and on the sentences just before and after it, *assumed* can best be interpreted as *taken*, or answer (D). Try to see it as a game. Which of the choices would best replace the word in question given its context, i.e., "a key role"? Choices (A), (B), (C), and (E) simply don't make sense given the gist of the paragraph.

12. D

In this question, you must remember that you are looking for the answer that is NOT correct. Referring directly to the passage for the answer, (A) can be found; it's a paraphrase of lines 25–26, which state that the first practical transformer *contain[ed] all the essential elements of the modern instrument.* Likewise, (B) and (C) can both be located in the passage in the discussion of the improvements in the transformer over the years (lines 24–30), and (E) is confirmed in line 35: *efficiency typically exceeds 99 percent.* The passage also confirms that (D) is NOT true: transformers today are said to be able to *handle…15 times the voltage* (lines 32–33) of earlier transformers, so (D) is the correct answer.

13. A

Here is another detail question. The first paragraph provides the information about the transformer that we need. A transformer, it says, *can convert electricity with a low current and a high voltage into electricity with a high current and low voltage* (lines 2–4). The passage goes on to state that this *conversion is important because electric power is transmitted most efficiently at high voltages* (lines 5–7). This information supports (A) as the best answer.

14. E

Inference questions simply ask you to recognize information in the passage that has been paraphrased or reworded. Here's how to find the answer to this question. The answer is found in the first sentence of the last paragraph. *Faraday demonstrated that in order for a magnetic field to induce a current in a conductor, the field must be changing* (lines 48–50). (E) is clearly the best answer. Of the wrong answers, (B), (C), and (D) are not true statements, because Oersted had nothing to do with the direct application of his findings, and Faraday did not invent the practical transformer. Only (A) is left, and it is also a misstatement; it's true about Oersted, not Faraday. Therefore, (E) is our best choice.

15. A

The author says that the Restoration plays were similar to the works of Shakespeare and his contemporaries in that both were popular, but they differed in that the Restoration plays focused on *the foibles of society, rather than the fortunes of kings and heroes* (lines 11–12). So, the author must think that the plays of Shakespeare focused on kings and heroes, as (A) indicates. Don't forget, there is a guessing penalty on the SAT, but eliminating answer choices can greatly improve you chances of guessing the correct answer.

16. B

It seems that the plays of the Restoration playwrights and Molière had similar subjects and themes. When the author writes that the British playwrights *took their cue from Molière,* (lines 7–8) you know that they were influenced by Molière in their work, or their artistic aims, as (B) states.

FOR MORE HELP...

Each question in this practice set deals primarily with one question type or one reading comprehension skill. Using the answers and explanations, find out what gave you the most difficulty. Then, use the table to find out where you can get even more practice with these skills. Kaplan's *The NEW SAT Critical Reading Workbook* is a great resource for additional practice.

Question Number	Type	Chapter	Chapter Topic
1	Two blanks question	3	Sentence Completion Practice Sets
2	One blank question	3	Sentence Completion Practice Sets
3	One blank question	3	Sentence Completion Practice Sets
4	Two blanks question	3	Sentence Completion Practice Sets
5	One blank question	3	Sentence Completion Practice Sets
6	Two blanks question	3	Sentence Completion Practice Sets
7	One blank question	3	Sentence Completion Practice Sets
8	Two blanks question	3	Sentence Completion Practice Sets
9	Detail question	4	Long Reading Comprehension Practice Sets

Question Number	Type	Chapter	Chapter Topic
10	Inference question	4	Long Reading Comprehension Practice Sets
11	Vocabulary-in-Context question	4	Long Reading Comprehension Practice Sets
12	Detail question	4	Long Reading Comprehension Practice Sets
13	Detail question	4	Long Reading Comprehension Practice Sets
14	Inference question	4	Long Reading Comprehension Practice Sets
15	Inference question	4	Short Reading Comprehension Practice Sets
16	Inference question	4	Short Reading Comprehension Practice Sets

The SAT Critical Reading section includes different passage types as well as different question types. To score your best, you need to be familiar with them. If you want to learn strategies that are targeted to the Critical Reading section, check out *The New SAT 2005 with CD-ROM* from Kaplan Test Prep and Admissions. This comprehensive book has tips, strategies, review lessons, as well as two full-length practice tests with detailed answer explanations.

Chapter Six: The New SAT Math Section

INTRODUCTION TO SAT MATH

The first thing you should know about SAT Math is how it's set up. If you can go in to the test knowing what to expect, it will give you confidence. There are three scored math sections: two 25-minute sections and one 20-minute section. These three sections are composed of Five-choice and Grid-in questions.

MULTIPLE-CHOICE QUESTIONS

This is the type of question you are probably most familiar with. It is simply a question followed by five answer choices. The correct answer is right in front of you—you just have to pick it out. The key to working quickly and efficiently through the Math section is to think about the question before you start looking for the answer.

GRID-INS

Just to reassure you, Grid-in questions test the same math concepts as multiple-choice questions. The only difference is that with Grid-ins, there are no answer choices. You have to calculate and fill in your own answer, in a special grid that looks like the one on the following page.

Grid-ins can really help you gain points because there is no penalty for wrong answers. If you get an answer wrong, you don't gain any points, but you don't lose points either. We advise that you never leave a Grid-in blank, because you have nothing to lose.

If you want to earn points, though, you'll need to make sure to fill in the grids correctly. The placement of your answer in the grid and how you grid tricky numbers such as fractions and decimals can determine whether you get a question right.

CALCULATORS AND THE SAT

If you didn't know—yes, you're allowed to use your calculator on the SAT. However, you don't ever *need* a calculator to solve an SAT Math question. Using your calculator will not always make problem solving easier. SAT Math questions test a lot more than your ability to do computations. Understanding when to use a calculator and when to leave it alone is critical on the SAT.

WRAPPING IT UP

Now you're ready to start practicing. We're giving you 18 questions covering a range of math topics and question types (Five-choice and Grid-in). Practice solving these questions and review the answer explanations found at the end of this chapter. By completing these practice questions, you'll be able to recognize your strengths and weaknesses, and you'll know exactly where to go for more help.

SAT MATH PRATICE SET

1. If x is the sum of n odd integers, which of the following must be true?

   (A) x is odd.

   (B) x is even.

   (C) $x \neq 0$

   (D) If x is even, n is even.

   (E) If x is odd, x is even.

2. If a speedboat travels at a rate of $\frac{x}{10}$ miles every y seconds, how many miles will the speedboat travel in z minutes?

   (A) $\dfrac{xy}{10z}$

   (B) $\dfrac{xz}{10y}$

   (C) $\dfrac{xyz}{10}$

   (D) $\dfrac{6xy}{z}$

   (E) $\dfrac{6xz}{y}$

3. If $|a + 3|$ and $|b - 2| = 4$, what is one possible value of $|a + b|$?

(A) −6

(B) −4

(C) 0

(D) 3

(E) 6

4. If $9^{2x-1} = 3^{3x+3}$, then $x =$

(A) −4

(B) $-\dfrac{7}{4}$

(C) $-\dfrac{10}{7}$

(D) 2

(E) 5

5. Twenty percent of the trees in an orchard are apple trees, and $\dfrac{1}{3}$ of the trees that are not apple trees are cherry trees. If $\dfrac{3}{4}$ of the trees in the orchard are fruit trees, and the only types of fruit trees in the orchard are apple trees, cherry trees, and plum trees, what fraction of the trees in the orchard are plum trees?

(A) $\dfrac{1}{30}$

(B) $\dfrac{3}{40}$

(C) $\dfrac{1}{12}$

(D) $\dfrac{17}{60}$

(E) $\dfrac{13}{45}$

6. $\dfrac{3\sqrt{3}}{\sqrt{2}} \times \dfrac{4\sqrt{3}}{3} =$

   (A) 3
   (B) $6\sqrt{2}$
   (C) 12
   (D) $12\sqrt{2}$
   (E) 36

7. If $x^2 - 9 < 0$, which of the following is true?
   (A) $x < -3$
   (B) $x > 3$
   (C) $x > 9$
   (D) $x < -3$ or $x > 3$
   (E) $-3 < x < 3$

Year	Income
1995	$20,000
1996	$25,000
1997	$30,000
1998	$33,000
1999	$36,000
2000	$44,000

8. The table above displays Jamie's income for each of the years 1995–2000. Which of the years 1996–2000 shows the greatest percent increase over the previous year?
   (A) 1996
   (B) 1997
   (C) 1998
   (D) 1999
   (E) 2000

9. If $f(x) = x^3 - x^2 - x$, what is the value of $f(-3)$?

  (A) -39

  (B) -33

  (C) -21

  (D) -15

  (E) 0

10. Five runners run in a race. The runners who come in first, second, and third place will win gold, silver, and bronze medals respectively. How many possible outcomes for gold, silver, and bronze medal winners are there?

  (A) 5

  (B) 10

  (C) 15

  (D) 30

  (E) 60

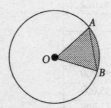

11. If $OA = AB = 6$ in the figure above, what is the area of the shaded region?

  (A) 36π

  (B) 12π

  (C) 6π

  (D) $9\sqrt{3}$

  (E) 18

12. $\overline{PQ}$ extends from $(-4, -8)$ to $(2, 10)$. Which of the following equations describes a line that intersects at its midpoint and is perpendicular to $\overline{PQ}$?

(A) $y = \dfrac{1}{3}x - \dfrac{1}{3}$

(B) $y = -\dfrac{1}{3}x + \dfrac{2}{3}$

(C) $y = -\dfrac{1}{3}x + \dfrac{2}{3}$

(D) $y = 3x - \dfrac{1}{3}$

(E) $y = 3x + \dfrac{2}{3}$

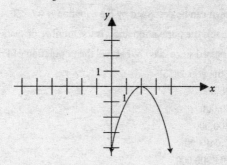

13. Which of the following equations best describes the curve shown in the graph above?

(A) $y = -x^2 + 2$
(B) $y = x^2 - 2$
(C) $y = (x + 2)^2$
(D) $y = (x - 2)^2$
(E) $y = -(x - 2)^2$

14. In the local chess club, the average age of the male members is 35 and the average age of the female members is 25. If 20 percent of the members are male, what is the average age of all the club members?

(A) 26

(B) 27

(C) 28

(D) 29

(E) 30

15. The population of Fridaville was 6,250 in the year 2000, and since then it has doubled every three years. The population of the town can be described by the equation $n = 6{,}250 \times (2^{\frac{t}{3}})$, where n is the population and t is the number of years that have passed since 2000. What will the population of Fridaville be in the year 2015?

(A) 20,000

(B) 50,000

(C) 200,000

(D) 2,048,000

(E) 204,800,000

16. The length of each side of square *A* is increased by 100 percent to make square *B*. If the length of each side of square *B* is increased by 50 percent to make square *C*, by what percent is the area of square *C* greater than the sum of the areas of squares *A* and *B*? (Disregard % sign when gridding your answer.)

17. A candy jar contains only grape, cherry, orange, and lemon candies. In the jar there are twice as many grape candies as cherry candies, and twice as many cherry candies as orange and lemon candies combined. If there are three times as many orange candies as lemon candies, what is the probability that a candy drawn at random from the jar will be an orange candy?

18. The expression $\dfrac{7x + 11}{5} - \dfrac{2x - 2}{5}$ is how much more than *x*?

ANSWERS AND EXPLANATIONS

1. D
You should try out a few possibilities since n could be even or odd. For instance, n could be 3, and all the odd integers could equal 1 for a sum of $x = 3$. Eliminate (B) and (E). Or, n could be 2 and all the odd integers could equal 1 for a sum of $x = 2$. Eliminate (A). Or, x could be the sum of -1 and 1; thus, $x = 0$ and choice (C) is out as well.

2. E
Since the problem involves a unit conversion from seconds to minutes, try substituting in numbers that do the converting for you. For instance, we could let $x = 20$ and $y = 60$, so that the speedboat travels $\frac{20}{10}$, or 2 miles every 60 seconds, or one minute. So, if we make $z = 2$ (the number of minutes), then the boat travels 2 miles a minute, so it must travel 4 miles in 2 minutes. So, 4 is your target number when $x = 20$, $y = 60$, and $z = 2$. Now, try out the answer choices.

(A) $\frac{xy}{10z} = \frac{20 \times 60}{10 \times 2}$, which is too large.

(B) $\frac{xz}{10y} = \frac{20 \times 2}{10 \times 60}$, which is too small.

(C) $\frac{xyz}{10} = \frac{20 \times 60 \times 2}{10}$, which is way too large.

(D) $\frac{6xy}{z} = \frac{6 \times 20 \times 60}{2}$, which is even larger.

(E) $\frac{6xz}{y} = \frac{6 \times 20 \times 2}{60} = 4$. We found it!

3. E

First, find all possible values of a and b. Then, find all possible values of $a + b$. Next, take the absolute value of each possible value of $a + b$, and see which answer choice matches one of the possibilities. Even before you calculate anything, you can rule out (A) and (B), since they are negative and $|a + b|$ must be non-negative.

$$|a + 3| = 1$$
$$a + 3 = 1 \text{ or } a + 3 = -1$$
$$a = -2 \text{ or } a = -4$$
$$b - 2 = 4 \text{ or } b - 2 = -4$$
$$b = 6 \text{ or } b = -2$$

The possible values of a are -2 and -4. The possible values of b are 6 and -2. These are the possible values of $a + b$.

$$-2 + 6 = 4$$
$$-2 + (-2) = -4$$
$$-4 + 6 = 2$$
$$-4 + (-2) = -6$$

Thus, the possible values of $a + b$ are -6, -4, 2, and 4.

Now $|-4| = 4$, $|-2| = 2$, $|4| = 4$, and $|6| = 6$. The possible values of $|a + b|$ are 2, 4, or 6. Choice (E), 6, is the only possible value of $|a + b|$ among the answer choices.

4. E

Rewrite the left side of the equation so that both sides have the same base:

$$9^{2x - 1} = 3^{3x + 3}$$
$$(3^2)^{2x - 1} = 3^{3x + 3}$$

When you raise a power to another power, you multiply the exponents, so you now have:

$$3^{4x - 2} = 3^{3x + 3}$$

Now that the bases are the same, just set the exponents to be equal:

$$4x - 2 = 3x + 3$$
$$4x - 3x = 3 + 2$$
$$x = 5$$

5. D

We'll treat this as we would any fraction problem with an unknown value, and plug in the largest denominator in the answer choices for the number of trees in the orchard. So, we'll assume there are 60 trees. Twenty percent, i.e., $\frac{1}{5}$ of these, or 12 of the trees, are apple trees, leaving 48 trees, of which $\frac{1}{3}$, or 16 trees, are cherry trees. $\frac{3}{4}$ of all the trees, or 45 trees, are fruit trees, and since all the fruit trees are either apple, cherry, or plum, that leaves $45 - (12 + 16) = 17$ plum trees. Thus, the fraction of all the trees in the orchard that are plum trees is $\frac{17}{60}$.

6. B

Without a calculator, this problem is challenging. But with one, it's pretty simple—if you use your parentheses correctly. The result you get is 8.485..., which doesn't seem to be among the answer choices. However, the correct answer should be more clear if you remember that the answer choices are nearly always in increasing or decreasing order. (A) is 3 and (C) is 12, so only (B) is in the right possible range. If you want to double check, calculate the value of (B) to compare.

7. E

Inequalities are being tested for the first time on the new SAT. Here's how you would solve this problem.

Rearrange $x^2 - 9 < 0$ to get $x^2 < 9$. We're looking for all the values of x that would fit this inequality. We need to consider both positive and negative values of x. Remember that $3^2 = 9$ and also that $(-3)^2 = 9$. If x is positive, and $x^2 < 9$, we can simply say that $x < 3$. But what if x is negative? x can take on only values whose square is less than 9. In other words, x cannot be less than or equal to -3. (Think of smaller numbers like -4 or -5; their squares are greater than 9.) So, if x is negative, then $x > -3$. x can also be 0. Therefore, $-3 < x < 3$. If you had trouble solving algebraically, you could have tried each answer choice:

(A) Say $x = -4$; $(-4)^2 - 9 = 16 - 9 = 7$. No good.

(B) Say $x = 4$; $4^2 - 9 = 16 - 9 = 7$. No good.

(C) Since 4 was too big, anything greater than 9 is too big. No good.

(D) Combination of (A) and (B), which were both wrong. No good.

Clearly, (E) must be correct.

8. A

The greatest dollar increase came in 1999–2000, but that's not necessarily the greatest percent increase. The $5,000 increase for 1995–96 is an increase of $\frac{1}{4}$, or 25%. The $5,000 increase the following year is an increase of just $\frac{1}{5}$, or 20%. You don't even have to give much thought to the $3,000 increases of the next 2 years—but what about the $8,000 increase in 1999–2000? $8,000 out of $36,000 is less than $\frac{1}{4}$, so there's no need to calculate the percent; the 1995–96 percent increase is the greatest.

9. B

Functions are new to the SAT in 2005. For this question, you can simply plug in −3 and see what you get.

$$f(x) = x^3 - x^2 - x$$
$$f(-3) = (-3)^3 - (-3)^2 - (-3)$$
$$= -27 - 9 + 3$$
$$= -33$$

10. E

Any of the 5 runners could come in first place, leaving 4 runners who could come in second place, leaving 3 runners who could come in third place, for a total of $5 \times 4 \times 3 = 60$ possible outcomes for gold, silver, and bronze medal winners.

11. C

Notice two sides of the triangle are radii. This means they must be the same length. So, $OB = OA = AB = 6$, which means the triangle is equilateral. Since all three angles of an equilateral triangle are 60 degrees, the shaded region must take up 60 degrees of the 360 degrees in the circle; in other words, $\frac{1}{6}$ of the circle ($\frac{60}{360} = \frac{1}{6}$). We know that the area of the entire circle is πr^2 or 36π. We want only $\frac{1}{6}$ of that though, which is 6π. So the area of the shaded region is 6π.

12. B

You will need to find the midpoint of $\overline{PQ}$ and its slope. You can then use the slope to find the slope of a line perpendicular to $\overline{PQ}$, and plug in the midpoint of $\overline{PQ}$ (since it is on the perpendicular line) to find the y-intercept of the line using the equation $y = mx + b$. Let the coordinates of the endpoints of a line segment be (x_1, y_1) and (x_2, y_2). The coordinates of the midpoint of this line segment are $\frac{x_1 + x_2}{2}, \frac{y_1 + y_2}{2}$.

$$\frac{x_1 + x_2}{2} = \frac{-4 + 2}{2} = \frac{-2}{2} = -1$$

$$\frac{y_1 + y_2}{2} = \frac{-8 + 10}{2} = \frac{2}{2} = 1$$

Midpoint of $\overline{PQ}$: $(-1, 1)$.

The slope m of a line passing through the points (x_1, y_1) and (x_2, y_2) is given by $m = \dfrac{y_2 - y_1}{x_2 - x_1}$.

Slope of $\overline{PQ}$: $\dfrac{10 - (-8)}{2 - (-4)} = \dfrac{18}{6} = 3$

The slope of any line perpendicular to $\overline{PQ}$ is $\dfrac{-1}{3}$, or $-\dfrac{1}{3}$.

Finding b: The equation of the line perpendicular to $\overline{PQ}$ is

$$y = \frac{1}{3}x + b.$$

$$1 = \frac{1}{3} + b$$

$$\frac{2}{3} = b$$

Equation of perpendicular line: $y = -\dfrac{1}{3}x + \dfrac{2}{3}$

13. E
If you recognize the shape in the graph and remember transposition rules, great, you can move straight to the answer. If you don't, though, just graph the 5 answer choices, one at a time on your calculator, and see which matches the curve shown.

14. B
This question contains a classic math trap. Here's how this math trap works.

The overall average is not simply the average of the average ages for male members and female members. Because there are a lot more females than males, females carry more weight, and the overall average age will be a lot closer to 25 than 35. This problem is easiest to deal with if you pick particular numbers for the females and males. The best numbers to pick are the smallest: Say there are 4 females and 1 male. Then, the ages of the 4 females are 4 times 25, or 100, and the age of the 1 male is 35. The average is $(100 + 35) \div 5$, or 27.

15. C

Find the number of years that have passed since 2000 and plug it into the equation to find *n*. Work carefully.

$$n = 6{,}250 \left(2^{\frac{15}{3}}\right) = 6{,}250 \times 2^5$$

$$= 6{,}250 \times 32 = 200{,}000$$

16. 80

The best way to solve this problem is to pick a value for the length of a side of square *A*. We want our numbers to be easy to work with, so let's pick 10 for the length of each side of square *A*. The length of each side of square *B* is 100 percent greater, or twice as great as a side of square *A*. So, the length of a side of square *B* is 2 × 10, or 20. The length of each side of square *C* is 50 percent greater, or $1\frac{1}{2}$ times as great as a side of square *B*. So, the length of a side of square *C* is $1\frac{1}{2}$ × 20 or 30. The area of square *A* is 10^2, or 100. The area of square *B* is 20^2, or 400. The sum of the areas of squares *A* and *B* is 100 + 400, or 500. The area of square *C* is 30^2, or 900. The area of square *C* is greater than the sum of the areas of squares *A* and *B* by 900 − 500, or 400. By what percent is the area of square *C* greater than the sum of the areas of squares *A* and *B*? $\frac{400}{500}$ × 100%, or 80%.

17. $\frac{3}{28}, \frac{6}{56}, \frac{9}{84}$ or .107

To answer this question, let's assume there is 1 lemon candy (since all the other numbers seem to build on this one). Read carefully through the question, and you'll see that that means there are 3 orange candies, 8 cherry candies, and 16 grape candies. So, the probability of picking an orange candy is:

$$\frac{\text{number of orange candies}}{\text{total number of candies}} = \frac{3}{1+3+8+16} = \frac{3}{28} \text{ or } .107$$

18. $\frac{13}{5}$ or 2.6

This problem may look funny at first because it's an algebra problem, and yet grid-in answers can't have variables. Here's one way to solve this question:

$$\frac{7x + 11}{5} - \frac{2x - 2}{5} = \frac{7x + 11 - (2x - 2)}{5} = \frac{5x + 13}{5} = \frac{5x}{5} + \frac{13}{5} =$$

$x + \frac{13}{5}$, which is $\frac{13}{5}$ more than x.

FOR MORE HELP...

Each question in this practice set deals primarily with one math topic. Using the answers and explanations, find out which math topics gave you the most difficulty. Then, use the following table to find out where you can get even more practice with these math skills. Kaplan's *The New SAT Math Workbook* is a great resource for additional math practice.

Question Number	Math Topic	Chapter(s)	Chapter Topic(s)
1	Number Properties	4	Number Properties
2	Rate	6	Ratios and Rates
3	Absolute Value	10	Basic Algebra
4	Exponents	8	Powers and Roots
5	Percents and Fractions	7	Percents
6	Roots	8	Powers and Roots
7	Inequalities	11	Advanced Algebra
8	Graphs	9	Graphs
9	Functions	11	Advanced Algebra
10	Outcomes	13	Logic Word Problems
11	Triangles, Circles, and Arcs	15, 17, 18	Triangles, Circles, Multiple Figures
12	Lines	14, 19	Lines and Angles, Coordinate Geometry

Question Number	Math Topic	Chapter(s)	Chapter Topic(s)
13	Quadratics	11	Advanced Algebra
14	Averages	5	Averages
15	Exponential Growth	3	Number Operations
16	Quadrilaterals	16	Quadrilaterals
17	Probability	13	Logic Word Problems
18	Algebra	10, 11	Basic Algebra, Advanced Algebra

Questions 1, 2, 5, 8, and 10–18 are word problems. Chapter twelve of *The New SAT Math Workbook* covers word problems.

The new SAT is going to include more advanced math topics. If you need to brush up on your math skills, or if you need tips and strategies for raising your score, *The New SAT 2005 with CD-ROM* is the book you need. Section IV of this book is devoted to the Math section, from basic strategies for answering multiple-choice and Grid-in questions, to the advanced math topics that will appear on the test. You will even learn about the SAT's math traps and how to avoid them.

Chapter Seven: **The New SAT Study Group Guide**

HOW TO TEAM UP FOR A BETTER SCORE ON THE SAT

Your first inclination in preparing for the SAT may be to work on your own, reading through Kaplan's SAT test prep books. It's true, using our books will improve your score. In fact, we guarantee it! However, when it comes to preparing for the SAT, there are several advantages to working as a group. Even if you cringe at the idea of a study group, you should think of all the advantages. (And if you can't think of any, just keep reading.) Besides, with the information in this chapter, we've made it easy to start a study group and reap all the advantages it has to offer.

Why Start an SAT Study Group?

- **An SAT Study Group keeps you committed.** You are far less likely to blow off studying if your friends are depending on you to show up at meetings and be useful.

- **An SAT Study Group helps you improve you skills.** It is sometimes hard to see your own weaknesses. Your SAT Study Group will help you recognize and correct your problem areas.

- **An SAT Study Group calms you down.** Preparing for the SAT can be stressful. It's no wonder some students get frazzled as test day approaches. Your SAT Study Group is there to give you the support you need.

Getting Started

The idea of a study group is to maximize your time, so don't waste precious hours planning the perfect study group. Use this checklist to get off to the right start.

- **Choose your Study Group wisely.** This doesn't mean you should team up only with straight-A students. It means you should find students who are serious about preparing for the SAT. Also you should consider finding members with different strengths and weaknesses. The SAT tests your reading, writing, and math skills, so you should find students who have different strengths in each of these skills. The right number of partners is important, too. We recommend limiting your group to three to six members. That way, you have all the benefits of teaming up, but no one gets overshadowed or left behind.

- **Set realistic goals.** Everyone in your Study Group should start by taking a practice test, such as those found in Kaplan's *The New SAT 2005*. Once each of you knows what your strengths and weaknesses are, you should have a discussion with your team about what you hope to gain from the SAT Study Group. For example, are you looking for an improved score? Or maybe reduced test anxiety? While it's important for each of you to have your own personal goals, a group will be successful only if it is working in the same general direction.

- **Find the right meeting place.** Most important, you are going to need a place where you can all sit comfortably for a couple of hours free from distraction. Some access to food and drinks is a nice bonus. Here are some other things you should keep in mind.

  Pick a location with:

  Good lighting. You have to be able to see and read all of your materials.

  Plenty of space for your materials. A large table or desk would be best for laying out your books and papers.

  Easy access for everyone in the group. It is not the best use of your time to spend an hour getting to and from each meeting.

  No restrictions on noise level. If you'd like to use your local library as a meeting place, ask your librarian if there is an area you can use without disturbing other patrons.

Chapter Seven | 79

- **Make a realistic schedule.** First, decide how often and for how long you are going to meet. We recommend at least four meetings of at least one hour each; two hours is better. It's hard to get anything accomplished in less time than this. Next, get out your calendars and mark down every meeting in advance. Commit to those times, but understand that sometimes things come up. One team member may have to miss a meeting because of an important sports match or because he gets sick. Make the best of these situations and try to stay on schedule, even if you are one member short. We also recommend that you decide in advance what material you will cover at each meeting.

SET A TIME LIMIT

By setting a start time and an end time, you force yourself to budget your minutes and use them wisely. It also keeps you from overtiring yourself. No one in the group wants to be the first one to "quit," which leads to never-ending, and ultimately unproductive meetings. Studying for hours on end won't improve your score—it will just burn you out. The members of your study group should agree to close their books at a set time so that you don't fall prey to study group burn out.

General Guidelines

OK, you know who, you know what, you know where, and you know when. But exactly *how* should you approach each meeting?

Set Small Goals

We've already discussed individual and team goals, but now it's time to set goals for each meeting. It's probably not helpful to say, "In this meeting, we're going to study SAT math." A goal that general will leave you feeling unaccomplished at the end of your meeting if, in fact, you don't review all the math topics found on the SAT. Get specific and set small goals so that throughout the meeting you can feel a sense of achievement. Try setting a goal to cover Grid-in strategies in the first half hour, or to review the algebra II topics that are appearing on the SAT for the first time in 2005 in the next hour. Even a small sense of accomplishment will boost your confidence.

Take Turns

Not everyone is great at the same things. Use this to your advantage in your SAT Study Group. If one of you is particularly good at recognizing and avoiding math traps, let him or her "teach" the rest of the group. Maybe one member of your group has an excellent vocabulary…ask him or her to present a brief lesson on using word roots, suffixes, and prefixes to decode words so that you can all improve your vocabulary and your score.

Aim for Variety

Taking turns will accentuate everyone's different strengths and weaknesses, but it will also help you from getting bored. Try to incorporate as much variety in your meetings as you can. For example, if you are reviewing for the multiple-choice questions on the Writing section, don't spend all your time reviewing Usage questions. Spend your time working on Usage, Sentence Correction, and Paragraph Correction questions so you won't get stuck in a studying rut.

Write On

Since essay writing is a completely new section on the SAT, and because it does not follow the typical multiple-choice format, your group will need to take a different approach to preparing for this section. First, choose a prompt. Next, take 25 minutes during your meeting and write a timed essay, just like you will have to write for the SAT. At the end of the 25 minutes (working as a group will keep you from taking extra time!), trade essays with members of your group. Read each other's essays and write down three things that are particularly strong about the essay, and three things that could be improved. Be specific and be constructive. Avoid making comments such as, "This essay is too general." Instead, try to make a suggestion about how this problem could be improved. For example, a comment such as, "Using specific details and information about your personal experience would make this essay much stronger," will be helpful. Finally, take these comments and apply them to the next essay you write.

Practice, Practice, Practice

Take at least one more practice test before test day. Try to take the practice test after a couple of meetings and discuss your results in a Study Group meeting. This will help you continue to pinpoint your trouble areas, gauge your progress, and build your familiarity with the test format. If you like, you can take another practice test after your last meeting to measure your improvement.

Don't Panic

A little stress before an exam will keep you focused on your goal, but if you are super-stressed, you won't think clearly and you won't perform well. Here are some of the ways you can keep stress levels in the Study Group to a minimum:

- **Work out with your SAT Study Group.** Exercise is an ideal stress reducer. Take an SAT Study Group partner—or your whole group—and take a quick walk around the block. Get together and go jogging or play basketball. Anything that gets your heart pounding for a little while will take the edge off your anxiety.

- **Compliment each other.** Sometimes it's hard to focus on the positive when you're stressed out. Make it an SAT Study Group activity for each group member to point out the strengths of other members (like "Celena is great with Critical Reading questions"). Do this regularly. You will see that new strengths will develop as you continue studying.

- **Celebrate together.** Don't forget to get together one last time after the test to celebrate a job well done!

What's the best way to prepare for the New SAT?

Create a study group!

Kaplan will even throw in a free* pizza party to help you get started.

How does the Kaplan NEW SAT Study Group Pizza Party work?

1. Purchase Kaplan's *The NEW SAT 2005* or Kaplan's *The NEW SAT 2005 with CD-ROM*, both of which include a Kaplan NEW SAT study group guide. Save your receipt as proof of purchase.

2. Fully complete the official request form below.

3. Mail the fully completed official request form plus your original Borders receipt for Kaplan's *The NEW SAT 2005* or Kaplan's *The NEW SAT 2005 with CD-ROM* as proof of purchase to: Kaplan/Simon & Schuster, 12th Floor, 1230 Avenue of the Americas, New York, NY 10020.

4. Kaplan will send you a gift certificate for a free Domino's large one-topping pizza and a 2-liter bottle of Coke® to use at one of your NEW SAT study group meetings.

*Get a gift certificate† for a free Domino's large one-topping pizza and a 2-liter bottle of Coke® when you submit your original receipt for Kaplan's *The NEW SAT 2005* or Kaplan's *The NEW SAT 2005 with CD-ROM* as proof of purchase and the fully completed official request form below. Please allow 10-12 weeks for delivery. Delivery cannot be guaranteed unless you include your zip code on the official request form. The Kaplan NEW SAT Study Group Pizza Party is valid in the U.S. (void in Puerto Rico) and Canada (void in Quebec) while supplies last. Offer may not be combined with any other offer. All Domino's Pizza® terms and conditions apply. Void where prohibited or otherwise restricted by law. All submissions become the property of Simon & Schuster and will not be returned. Simon & Schuster is not responsible for lost, late, illegible, incomplete, postage-due or misdirected forms or mail. Requests not complying with all offer requirements will not be honored. Approximate retail value of Kaplan NEW SAT Study Group Pizza Party is $14.00. Offer ends the earlier of January 12, 2005 or while supplies last. All request forms must be received no later than January 12, 2005.

†Domino's Pizza® gift certificate valid at participating locations only. For a store near you, visit **www.dominos.com**.

- -

Kaplan NEW SAT Study Group Pizza Party Official Request Form

I am enclosing my sales receipt of Kaplan's *The NEW SAT 2005* or Kaplan's *The NEW SAT 2005 with CD-ROM* as proof of purchase. Please send me my gift certificate for a free Domino's large one-topping pizza and a 2-liter bottle of Coke® for my Kaplan NEW SAT Study Group Pizza Party.

Name _____

Address _____

City _____ State _____ Zip _____

KAPLAN
Test Prep and Admissions
Published by Simon & Schuster

BORDERS.
BOOKS MUSIC MOVIES CAFE

Save up to $10 when you purchase Kaplan guides to the New SAT!

You are eligible for a $2.00 publisher rebate with the purchase of each of the following Kaplan titles:

- *The NEW SAT 2005 with CD-ROM*
- *The NEW SAT Math Workbook*
- *The NEW SAT Writing Workbook*
- *The NEW SAT Critical Reading Workbook*
- *NEW SAT 2400*

Simply complete the **publisher mail-in rebate coupon below**, attach it to the **original Borders receipt for your Kaplan SAT guides** as proof of purchase, mail it to Simon & Schuster Customer Service, and we'll send you $2 for each eligible title purchased. Rebate must be redeemed through the publisher. Reduction not taken at point of purchase.

Please Send Me My Kaplan SAT Guide Publisher Rebate!

I am enclosing:

1. this completed mail-in publisher rebate coupon.
2. the original Borders receipt for my Kaplan SAT guides as proof of purchase. (Rebates will not be processed without sales receipt.)

Number of eligible titles purchased _____ × $2.00 = _____
Name (to whom check should be made payable):

Address: _____

City/State/Zip: _____

Telephone: _____   Email address: _____

Mail this coupon and your original receipt to:
Simon & Schuster Customer Service
Kaplan SAT Guide Rebate
100 Front Street
Riverside, NJ 08075-1197

KAPLAN

Test Prep and Admissions

Save $50 on Kaplan's New SAT Course!

By purchasing this book, you've taken the first step toward scoring higher on the New SAT. After you've assessed your skills and determined your score goals, we'll give you a $50 discount on Kaplan's classroom course for the New SAT – the most powerful, up-to-date preparation program for the new test. Prefer to prepare online? We'll give you $25 off the cost of Kaplan's online course for the New SAT.

Simply complete the form, send it to Kaplan with your Borders receipt as proof of purchase, and we'll send you a personal confirmation code making you eligible to receive a $50 discount for a classroom course or a $25 discount for an online course.

If you decide to register for a New SAT course, call 1-800-KAP-TEST to enroll. Be sure to tell our representative that you have a confirmation code for a New SAT course discount. *Important: You must provide your confirmation code when you register. If you register for a course before receiving your confirmation code, you will not be eligible for a discount.*

Yes! I'd like a discount on Kaplan's New SAT course!

I am enclosing my Borders sales receipt as proof of purchase. Please send me my personal confirmation code, entitling me to a $50 discount on Kaplan's New SAT classroom course, or a $25 discount on Kaplan's New SAT online course.

PLEASE NOTE: The name provided here must be the name of the student interested in the Kaplan course.

Name (to whom check should be made payable): _____

Address: _____

City/State/Zip: _____

Telephone: _____   Email address: _____

❑ Check here to receive Kaplan's free email newsletter with test-taking tips, admissions info, and more!

Complete the form and return with your receipt to: **Simon & Schuster, 1230 Avenue of the Americas, 12th floor, New York, NY 10020.**